24-25

D1459892

MAR   2002

GEORGIA

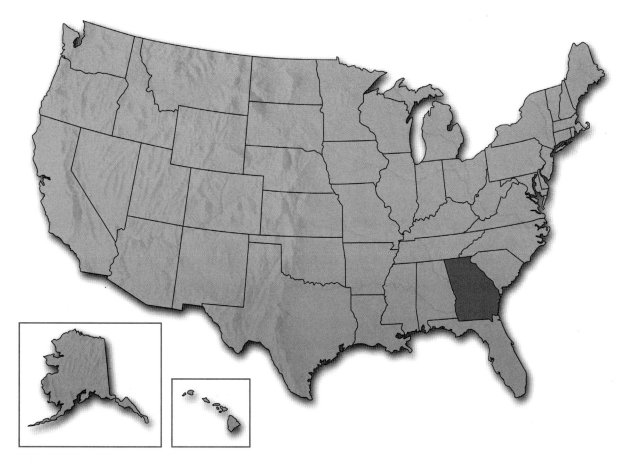

Jennifer Nault

Published by Weigl Publishers Inc.
123 South Broad Street, Box 227
Mankato, MN   56002
USA
Web site: http://www.weigl.com

Library of Congress Cataloging-in-Publication Data

Nault, Jennifer.
    Georgia / Jennifer Nault.
        p. cm. -- (A kid's guide to American states)
    Includes bibliographical references (p.) and index.
    ISBN 1-930954-28-X
     1. Georgia--Juvenile literature. [1. Georgia.] I. Title. II. Series.

F286.3 .N38 2001

2001017992

ISBN 1-930954-71-9 (pbk.)

Printed in the United States of America
1 2 3 4 5 6 7 8 9 10   05 04 03 02 01

Project Coordinator
Michael Lowry
Copy Editor
Bryan Pezzi
Designers
Warren Clark
Terry Paulhus
Photo Researcher
Diana Marshall

Photograph Credits

Cover: Athens' double barrel cannon on lawn of City Hall (Athens Convention &
Visitors Bureau), Peaches (Corel Corporation); **Athens Convention & Visitors
Bureau:** pages 21T, 28B; **City of Atlanta/The Atlanta Cyclorama:** page 24BL;
CNP/Archive Photos: page 21BR; **Columbus Convention & Visitors Bureau:** page
20B; **Corel Corporation:** pages 11B, 15BL; **Dave Dennis/Tom Stack & Associates:**
page 7BL; **Digital Stock Corporation:** page 29B; **Georgia Department of Industry,
Trade & Tourism Image Library:** pages 3M, 3B, 4T, 4BR, 5T, 5BL, 6T, 6B, 7T, 8BL, 9T,
10T, 10BL, 10BR, 11T, 12T, 12BL, 12BR, 13T, 13B, 14T, 14B, 15BR, 16T, 16B, 18BL,
19B, 20T, 22T, 22BR, 22BL, 24T, 24BR, 25B, 27T, 27BL, 27BR, 28T, 29T; **Georgia
Department of Natural Resources:** pages 3T, 8T, 8BR, 17BL; **Courtesy of the Georgia
Historical Society:** pages 18T, 18BR, 19T; **Georgia Secretary of State:** page 4BL; **Helen
Convention & Visitors Bureau:** page 23BL; © **Wally McNamee/CORBIS:** page 26B;
PhotoDisc, Inc.: pages 9B, 15T; **Photofest:** pages 25T, 26T; © **Flip Schulke/CORBIS:**
page 7BR; **Theatre Gael:** page 23T; **Visuals Unlimited, Inc.:** page 21BL; **Marilyn
"Angel" Wynn:** pages 17T, 17BR, 23BR.

CONTENTS

Introduction 4

Land and Climate 8

Natural Resources 9

Plants and Animals 10

Tourism 12

Industry 13

Goods and Services 14

First Nations 16

Explorers and Missionaries 18

Early Settlers 19

Population 20

Politics and Government 21

Cultural Groups 22

Arts and Entertainment 24

Sports 26

Brain Teasers 28

For More Information 30

Glossary 31

Index 32

Built for the 1996 Olympic Games, Atlanta's Centennial Olympic Park features a water fountain of the five Olympic Rings.

INTRODUCTION

Georgia is known as "The Empire State of the South." This nickname refers to Georgia's role as the center of agricultural and industrial development in the South. The state was once the cotton capital of the nation, and cotton is still one of its main industries. In Georgia's early days, those who owned **plantation** homes were known for their wealth and their fine southern manners. Early Georgians were proud and friendly people—a tradition that continues today.

Georgia's landscape is a dramatic combination of bayous, beaches, mountains, and plains. The state is decorated with moss-covered trees, colorful magnolias, and majestic pines. In fact, the expression "tall as a Georgia pine" came from the state's giant pine trees.

The Reynolds Mansion, like many other plantation homes in Georgia, is rich in southern history. Built between 1807 and 1810, it represents the success of the sugarcane and cotton industries.

QUICK FACTS

Georgia's state flower, the Cherokee rose, has a legend attached to it. Cherokee mothers wept when settlers forced them off their land. The legend claims that a rose grew wherever their tears had fallen.

The design of Georgia's state flag developed over time. The current flag contains images of Georgia's three previous flags. The latest design was adopted on January 30, 2001.

The right whale is Georgia's state marine mammal. This **endangered** creature can grow up to 50 feet in length and is the only great whale that is native to Georgia's coastal waters.

On average, there are 2,400 flights departing and arriving daily at the Hartsfield-Atlanta International Airport.

Getting There

Georgia is located in the Deep South of the United States. The southeastern corner of the state skims the Atlantic Ocean, with several islands located just offshore. Georgia is bordered by Florida to the south, Alabama to the west, Tennessee and North Carolina to the north, and South Carolina to the east.

Georgia is home to 304 airports, with the Hartsfield-Atlanta International Airport serving as the state's main airport. In fact, the Hartsfield-Atlanta International Airport is the second-busiest airport in the country. Georgia also has many roads, railroads, and highways, which allow easy access to this charming state.

QUICK FACTS

The Savannah River forms Georgia's eastern boundary with South Carolina. The Chattahoochee River forms the state's western boundary with Alabama.

As a result of its large peanut industry, Georgia has earned the nickname "The Goober State." In Georgia, "goober" is another word for "peanut."

Georgia's state wildflower is the azalea. This colorful flower can be found across the state.

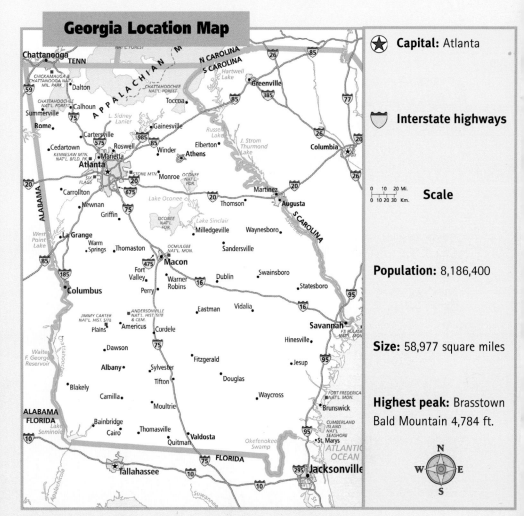

Georgia Location Map

⭐ **Capital:** Atlanta

🛡️ **Interstate highways**

Scale
0 10 20 Mi.
0 10 20 30 Km.

Population: 8,186,400

Size: 58,977 square miles

Highest peak: Brasstown Bald Mountain 4,784 ft.

Southern homes combine various architectural styles, including covered balconies, French doors, and Greek columns.

The colony of Georgia was founded in 1733 and was named after Great Britain's King George II. Georgians were among the first to sign the Declaration of Independence. On January 2, 1788, Georgia became a state. It was the first southern state to join the Union.

Georgia's warm history of southern generosity is offset by its long history of slavery and its economic decline during the American Civil War. Many Georgians believed that they had the right to own slaves. On January 19, 1861, Georgians voted to **secede** from the Union and join the other southern states to form the Confederate States of America. Georgia suffered enormously during the American Civil War, and many Georgians were killed or imprisoned. In November of 1864, Union soldiers set fire to Atlanta and destroyed the countryside during the **March to the Sea**. While the American Civil War put an end to slavery in Georgia, it also severely damaged the state's economy. It was some time before Georgia's economy and spirit strengthened again.

QUICK FACTS

Georgia's official state song is "Georgia on My Mind." Hoagy Carmichael composed the tune, and Stuart Gorrell wrote the words.

Quartz was chosen as the official state gem in 1976. Quartz comes in a variety of colors and can be found throughout the state.

Georgia's state motto is "Wisdom, Justice, and Moderation; Agriculture and Commerce." It was introduced in 1776.

Georgia was one of the original thirteen British colonies. It was the fourth state to join the Union.

During the American Civil War, Georgia was one of the main providers of food, weapons, and other supplies for the Confederate Army.

Atlanta is often described as a horizontal city. Since it has few natural barriers to prevent its outward growth, it has expanded outward instead of upward.

In the second half of the twentieth century, African Americans in Georgia and throughout the country began to ask for equal treatment. They were against **segregation**. The practice of segregation kept African Americans separate from the rest of the population. The **civil rights movement** of the 1960s sought to bring equal rights to African Americans. Atlanta was at the heart of this movement. Martin Luther King Jr. advised African Americans to work towards equal rights in a peaceful manner. It took much effort, but the movement helped reverse racial inequality in the United States.

QUICK FACTS

When Abraham Lincoln became president, Georgia declared itself a free republic and left the Union. Many Georgians were afraid that they would lose their plantations if Abraham Lincoln outlawed slavery. Georgia was readmitted to the Union in 1870.

The state insect is the honeybee. Georgia also has a state butterfly—the tiger swallowtail.

Today, more than 8.1 million people call Georgia home. Atlanta is Georgia's largest city and also its state capital. Atlanta is the state's financial, industrial, and transportation center. Atlanta is also known as the business capital of the southeastern United States.

Martin Luther King Jr. was born in "Sweet Auburn," the African-American center of Atlanta. It was here that he developed a passion for equality and tolerance.

Georgia has 1,011 square miles of inland water.

LAND AND CLIMATE

Similar to other states in the Deep South, Georgia has many swamps and marshes. Ridges and mountains cover the state's northern region and gradually flatten into rolling hills in the south. The Atlantic Coastal Plain and the Gulf Coastal Plain make up the largest portion of the state, about 60 percent. They extend through the southern part of the state to the Atlantic Ocean. The Blue Ridge and the Ridge and Valley regions are in the Appalachian Highlands. These areas are mountainous, made up of hard, folded rock.

Georgia's southern location makes for mild winters, with snow rarely falling beyond the northern counties. Georgia's summers are known to be very hot and humid. In the summer, the temperature ranges from 78° Fahrenheit in the northwest to 81°F in the southeast. January's average temperature in the southeast is a mild 54°F, whereas the northwest dips down to 44°F. Temperatures in Georgia rarely reach the freezing point. Georgia receives 44 to 68 inches of **precipitation** per year.

The Reed Bingham State Park attracts many tourists each year. Visitors come to fish, canoe, and water-ski on the lake.

NATURAL RESOURCES

Forests are one of Georgia's most important natural resources. The state is home to 24 million acres of commercial forests. Forestry is a thriving industry that employs about 34,000 people. Georgian trees provide various industries with raw materials. The state is a leader in the production of turpentine. This sticky liquid is found in some cone-bearing trees. Turpentine is a well-known paint thinner, but it is also used in medicines. Georgia supplies a large amount of lumber and **pulpwood** to the nation. There are many pulp and paper mills scattered throughout the state.

Georgia is an important source of stone and clay. The state supplies several types of clay, such as kaolin. These clays are removed from large, open-pit mines. Clay is used to make paper, paint, plastic, and rubber. Marble and granite are both **quarried** in Georgia.

Georgia is home to twenty-seven pulp and paper mills. The state produces more paper and paperboard than any other state, except Alabama.

Georgia is the leading producer of kaolin in the United States. Kaolin is one of the key ingredients in latex paint.

QUICK FACTS

Pickens County in northern Georgia is the site of one of the world's largest deposits of marble.

Georgia has the largest number of commercial forests in the United States.

Scientist Charles H. Herty came up with a discovery for the use of Georgia's pine trees. He developed a way to make kraft paper, fine white paper, and plastics out of these trees.

Georgia's fifty-nine state parks protect the lush plant life that is a result of the state's hot, humid climate.

PLANTS AND ANIMALS

Georgia's forests and woodlands take up about 65 percent of the state's total land area. Trees common to the state are birch, ash, sweet gum, sycamore, bald cypress, sassafras, cottonwood, and pine. Near the coast, the undergrowth consists of shrubs, vines, and palmettos. These short plants thrive in the shade of larger trees. Palmettos grow well in sandy soils, whereas bald cypresses and tupelo gums grow in swampy areas.

Georgia's balmy climate and fertile soils allow many kinds of flowers to flourish. Flowers native to Georgia include may apple, bellwort, trillium, violet, daisy, Japanese honeysuckle, lady slipper, and hepatica.

The Confederate daisy, also called the "Stone Mountain yellow daisy," can only be found within a 60-mile radius of Georgia's Stone Mountain.

QUICK FACTS

The live oak, which is the state tree, prospers in the southern region of the coastal plains.

There are fifty endangered plant species in the state.

Floating lily pads and wild orchids grow in the fertile waters of Okefenokee Swamp. Thick Spanish moss covers the swamp's many cypress trees.

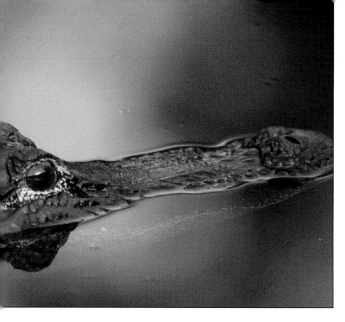

There are an estimated 10,000 to 13,000 alligators living in the Okefenokee National Wildlife Refuge.

There is a wide range of wildlife in Georgia. In the forests, there are black bears, gray squirrels, flying squirrels, muskrats, gray and red foxes, and raccoons. The white-tailed deer is the most common large animal in the state. Georgia's many swamps and rivers are home to beavers and otters. In the south, alligators, turtles, crabs, and shrimps inhabit the coastal waters. Fish in Georgia's lakes and rivers include rainbow trout, shad, catfish, eel, and bass.

Many kinds of birds can be found within the state. **Game** birds include quail, ruffed grouse, marsh hens, ducks, and wild turkeys. Smaller songbirds can be found chirping in the state as well. Among them are wood thrushes, mockingbirds, and brown thrashers. Human contact and natural predators have taken a toll on Georgia's wildlife. Twenty animal species are listed as endangered in the state.

Georgia's warm climate makes a good permanent home for the mourning dove, which can be found in the state throughout the year.

The Confederate Memorial Carving depicts Confederate President Jefferson Davis and Generals Robert E. Lee and Thomas J. Jackson.

QUICK FACTS

Tourists can visit President Franklin D. Roosevelt's summer home, called Little White House. People bathe in the waters of nearby Warm Springs, believing that the waters have healing powers.

Tourism is the second-largest industry in Georgia. Tourists spend about $18 billion in the state per year.

Atlanta's SciTrek Museum fascinates visitors with its imaginative science exhibits.

TOURISM

Visitors to Georgia can learn about southern culture and history by exploring some of the state's many historic sites. Historic forts and monuments re-create Georgia's American Civil War history. The image of three Confederate leaders is carved into Stone Mountain near Atlanta. Andersonville National Historic Site is another attraction. This memorial honors the Union soldiers who were held captive in the Andersonville prison during the American Civil War. Recently, the National Prisoner of War Museum opened up in Georgia. Visitors can learn what life was like for prisoners during the American Civil War.

Tourists also come to visit Georgia's popular seaside resorts. Some of these resorts rent sailboats, sea kayaks, and other sea crafts, allowing vacationers to participate in a variety of water sports. Many people come to the state to fish the ocean for flounder, bass, and trout. Inland lakes and streams also provide fishers with great catches.

St. Simons Island offers more than just sailing. Visitors can also take a 75-minute dolphin tour by boat of the area. On these adventures, tourists learn about the state's aquatic animals.

The museum at the Historic Cotton Exchange Welcome Center displays farm tools from Georgia's early cotton industry.

QUICK FACTS

Most of Georgia's electricity comes from the burning of fossil fuels. Nuclear power plants and **hydroelectric** plants supply the rest of the state's electricity.

Georgia's main exports include wood pulp, paper products, and clay. Its chief imports include chemicals, petroleum, iron, steel, and food products.

INDUSTRY

Before the 1900s, Georgia's economy was largely dependent upon cotton. The state's many cotton plantations prospered for more than a century. Although cotton production brought money into the state, the history of Georgia's early cotton plantations is marked by controversy. African-American slaves were made to work in the cotton fields. In the 1920s, cotton crops were ravaged by a beetle called the boll weevil. It caused incredible damage to the state's cotton crops. After farming practices were developed to control the beetle, the cotton industry began to recover.

Today, cotton still contributes to Georgia's economy, but more money is made from industries that turn cotton into finished products. Cotton **textile** production is a booming industry, and many textile mills experiment in making new kinds of fabrics for consumers. Commonly manufactured fabrics include velvet, denim, terry cloth, and corduroy. Other items manufactured in the state include paper, automobiles, mobile homes, airplanes, processed foods, and chemicals.

The cotton industry employs more than 53,000 Georgians on farms, in warehouses, and in textile mills.

GOODS AND SERVICES

Georgia is the third-largest producer of peaches in the United States. Peaches are harvested between mid-May and mid-August.

Georgia farms provide their citizens with corn, peanuts, pecans, and soybeans. Georgia has earned the nickname "The Peach State" for the huge number of peaches that are grown in the state. Georgia is one of the nation's leading producers of this fuzzy fruit. The state's fertile soil is also responsible for producing many of the country's watermelons and cantaloupes.

One of the most well-known products to be manufactured in Georgia is a soft drink. In 1886, Dr. John S. Pemberton invented Coca-Cola in Atlanta. This celebrated beverage was first sold out of a soda fountain in Jacob's Pharmacy. The name and logo were suggested by Dr. Pemberton's bookkeeper, Frank Robinson.

QUICK FACTS

The poultry industry has grown rapidly over the past few years. Georgia provides many **broiler chickens** and turkeys to the nation.

Food processing is an important industry in Georgia. Industries freeze and can fruits, vegetables, and shrimps.

Georgia grows 6 percent of the tobacco used in the United States.

Coca-Cola products are served in more than 195 countries around the world. The Coca-Cola symbol is the most well-known trademark in the world. It is recognized by 94 percent of Earth's population.

The World of Coca-Cola is a three-story pavilion in downtown Atlanta. The well-known soft drink was invented in Atlanta more than 110 years ago.

The **Atlanta-Fulton Public Library System** has 2.4 million books, 42,428 audio cassettes, 23,065 compact discs, and 48,734 videos, all of which are available to the public.

Manufacturing is Georgia's most profitable industry, while the state's service industry employs the most people.

Georgia's first newspaper was the *Georgia Gazette*. James Johnston started publishing this newspaper in 1763.

Georgia is responsible for 40 percent of all peanuts grown in the United States. The state has 6,000 peanut farmers.

Georgia's citizens can access information and education in a variety of ways. There are many public schools in Georgia, and attendance is required by law for young people between the ages of 7 and 16 years. In Georgia's early days, children were educated in tiny cabins. Since some Georgians live in small, mountain communities, schools have been built to educate those in isolated areas. Sometimes schools in these remote areas have few students.

The University of Georgia, which was created in 1785, is the state's largest university. Located in Athens, it is the oldest **state-chartered** university in the nation. It is considered the birthplace of higher education in the United States.

Residents of Georgia may access more than 250 newspapers to read up on state and world events. Book lovers can visit one of Georgia's fifty-three libraries, which serve cities and towns throughout the state.

The University of Georgia's main campus, in Athens, covers 605 acres of land and contains 313 buildings.

FIRST NATIONS

Two of the largest artifacts left by the Mound Builders were unearthed at the Etowah Indian Mounds in Cartersville.

The Paleo-Indians were the first people to inhabit what is now Georgia, more than 10,000 years ago. These hunters used shaved flint arrowheads to catch large prey. Since they hunted animals that moved from place to place, the Paleo-Indians did not stay long in one area. It was thousands of years before people started permanent settlements in the region.

The Woodland culture existed between 1000 BC and 900 AD. The Woodland society developed agricultural skills that allowed them to settle on the land. Crops and a variety of wild foods kept them fed when prey was scarce. The Woodland culture is known for the massive mounds they built in the area. These mounds earned them the name "Mound Builders." The mounds were large, long hills that were made from clay and earth. Many mounds contained human remains, jewelry, figurines, and pottery. Some of the mounds were made in the shapes of animals. One of Georgia's many mounds is shaped like a large bird and is known as Rock Eagle.

The Etowah Indian Mounds once marked the home of several thousand Native Americans. The largest of these mounds is over 63 feet high and covers 3 acres of land.

Chief Sequoyah's Cherokee alphabet was made up of eighty-five characters.

QUICK FACTS

When the United States Congress passed the "Indian Removal Act," many of the last remaining Cherokee were driven out of Georgia.

The Creek are believed to be direct **descendants** of the Mound Builders.

The path that the Cherokee took from Georgia to the west side of the Mississippi River is called the Trail of Tears. About 4,000 people died on this forced journey west. Today, the New Echota Historic Site marks the starting point of that journey.

New Echota Historic Site

The Cherokee and the Creek were living in the Georgia area when the Europeans arrived. They were great farmers, growing mainly pumpkins, beets, corn, and squashes. By the time the British made Georgia a colony, very few Cherokee and Creek remained. Many had died from new diseases brought by the Europeans, who had begun exploring the area in the mid-1500s. The Cherokee and the Creek became ill with smallpox and measles, which were almost always fatal. Between 1500 and 1700, at least half of the Native Americans in the area died.

The Cherokee that survived maintained their rich culture, as well as their own alphabet. Chief Sequoyah invented a Cherokee alphabet and taught his people to read and write. For a time, the Cherokee had their own government, constitution, and newspaper. In the 1830s, the United States government forced the Cherokee to move out of Georgia to **reservations** on the west side of the Mississippi River.

Chief Tomochichi, of the Creek, formed a treaty with James Edward Oglethorpe in 1733. The treaty allowed for the peaceful settlement of Savannah, Georgia's first town.

EXPLORERS AND MISSIONARIES

Hernando de Soto was the first European to arrive in Georgia. This well-known Spanish explorer arrived in 1540. In 1566, another Spanish explorer, Pedro Menéndez de Avilés, founded a fort and mission on Saint Catherines Island, off Georgia's coast. The Spanish built many more forts and missions along the coast. They called this area Guale. The majority of Guale's settlers were Franciscan missionaries, who sought to **convert** Native Americans to the Roman Catholic religion. At one point, the Franciscans had thirty-eight missions in the region.

King Charles I of England claimed Georgia in 1629. Although it was a struggle, the British won full ownership of the area in 1686 with the help of Native Americans. Still, the British had to fight the Spanish for another seventy years to keep Georgia.

Savannah was the first North American city to be planned on a system of square blocks.

During the 1500s, Hernando de Soto led a group of 600 Spanish soldiers, merchants, and priests on a journey through Georgia, looking for gold.

QUICK FACTS

King Charles I wanted the colony of Georgia to produce wine, silk, and other goods for the British Empire.

During the time that the Spanish and the British fought for control of Georgia, it became known as the Debatable Land.

Savannah was the first British settlement in Georgia. It was founded in 1733.

James Edward Oglethorpe was the founder of the colony of Georgia. He is the only colonial governor to have never owned a single acre of state land.

EARLY SETTLERS

After the British took Georgia from Spain, many British settlers began moving to the area. King George II granted a charter to a British soldier, James Edward Oglethorpe, allowing him to start a colony for Britain's poor. Oglethorpe planned to create a perfect society, where poor British citizens who owed money or faced prison terms could have a second chance. Oglethorpe's vision was for a land where no one was rich or poor. People who were sent to Georgia by the British government were given supplies and 50 acres of land. Those who were able to pay their own way were given 500 acres of land.

Many early settlers lived along the Savannah River. Some of the British who settled the region grew tobacco and cotton. Others made wines and silks, and grew spices. These products were shipped back to Britain so that the British would not have to buy these goods from other countries. This system was called **mercantilism**.

QUICK FACTS

James Edward Oglethorpe described Georgia as "serene, pleasant, and temperate, never subject to excessive heat or cold."

The Indian Springs State Park has a mineral spring that was used by the Creek hundreds of years ago.

In 1735, Georgia passed laws that outlawed alcohol and slavery. While these laws disappeared over time, Georgia was once the only British colony in North America with such laws.

The success of Georgia's plantation farms was a result of the labor of the state's African-American slaves.

In the late 1800s, the Hofwyl-Broadfield Plantation consisted of 7,300 acres of land for rice cultivation. Today, visitors can tour the historic site to learn about plantation life for the owners and the 357 African-American slaves who worked the fields.

POPULATION

More than one-quarter of Georgia's population is under 18 years of age.

QUICK FACTS

Georgia is the country's tenth-largest state by population.

In the 1980s, Georgia was one of the nation's fastest-growing states in population.

Other large cities in the state include Columbus and Savannah.

African Americans and people of European descent make up the largest portion of Georgia's population. There are very few Asian, Native-American, or Hispanic-American citizens living in Georgia. People of European heritage make up about 71 percent of the population, with many of Irish, British, and German descent. About 27 percent of the state's residents are African Americans. The African-American population in the state has declined since 1860, when African Americans made up nearly one-half of Georgia's population.

Nearly 63 percent of Georgia's citizens live in urban areas. Approximately two-fifths of the population resides in Atlanta. About 404,000 people live in the city, and 3.5 million live in the surrounding areas.

The city of Columbus was planned along the banks of the Chattahoochee River in the early 1800s. The 12-mile Riverwalk is one of the city's most notable features.

The original Athens-Clarke County City Hall once housed a ground-floor market.

POLITICS AND GOVERNMENT

Throughout history, Georgia's citizens have favored the Democratic Party. In fact, all of the state's governors were Democrats from 1872 until 1964. Since 1964, the Democrats have remained quite strong, but the Republican Party has also won some elections.

Georgia is divided into 159 counties, and boards of commissioners govern 156 of them. The remaining three counties are governed by the local judge. Commissioners take care of local governing. Most commissioners are elected, and a few are appointed. Once in power, commissioners serve their counties for four-year terms. Georgia's General Assembly is made up of two branches—the Senate and the House of Representatives. The Senate has 56 members, and the House of Representatives has 180 members. The state's governor has much control over Georgia's finances. During the governor's four-year term, he or she is also the director of the state budget.

QUICK FACTS

The first African-American mayor of Atlanta was Maynard Jackson. He served three successful terms as mayor of Atlanta. It was under his leadership that Atlanta secured the 1996 Olympic Games.

Jimmy Carter, who was governor of Georgia, later served as the nation's thirty-ninth president. Jimmy Carter was the first Georgian to hold this title. People can visit his home at The Jimmy Carter National Historic Site in Plains.

Maynard Jackson was mayor of Atlanta from 1974 to 1982, and again from 1990 to 1994. Many people credit him with making the city the thriving business center it is today.

The Apex Museum, in Atlanta, displays art and artifacts from ancient African civilizations to present-day African-American culture.

CULTURAL GROUPS

From African art to gospel choirs, Georgia is rich in African-American culture. Museums and galleries throughout the state keep the African-American heritage alive. The Morton Theater in Athens played an important role in the development of African-American music in the 1920s. It is believed that jazz greats such as Duke Ellington, Bessie Smith, and Louis Armstrong played on its stage.

In 1968, Coretta Scott King established the Martin Luther King Center in Atlanta. The King Center is a living memorial to the work of Martin Luther King Jr. Visitors to the King Center include foreign leaders and international tourists, representing different cultures, races, and religions.

QUICK FACTS

The Tubman African American Museum celebrates Georgia's African-American art, history, and culture.

Every year more than 1 million visitors come to the Martin Luther King Center in Atlanta to pay tribute to King and his legacy.

Many Georgian African Americans are of the Baptist faith. Over half of Georgia's church members are Baptists.

Gospel singing is often accompanied by organ music, hand clapping, and tambourines.

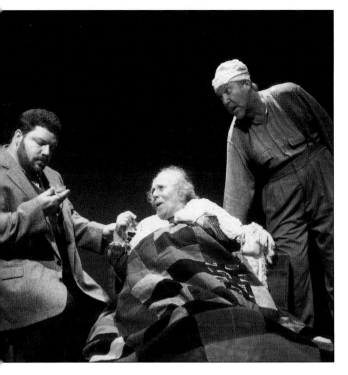

The Theatre Gael was founded in 1984 to preserve the traditions and stories of Celtic culture in Georgia.

One in five Georgians can trace their ancestry back to Ireland, Scotland, or Wales. The Theatre Gael in Atlanta is devoted to producing and preserving the plays, poetry, music, dance, and storytelling of Celtic culture. At the theater, Celtic Americans are given a chance to discover their rich heritage.

While Native Americans make up only a small percentage of Georgia's population, there are still many events throughout the state that celebrate their culture. At the Tifton Native American Cultural Exchange, there are displays on Native-American history, hunting techniques, tools and weapons, tepees, and storytelling. Native-American dancers also perform and talk about the meanings behind their costumes and dances.

QUICK FACTS

During the civil rights movement, protestors peacefully marched around places that practiced segregation.

The Cherokee of Georgia hold an Annual Spring Powwow in Saint George.

The town of Helen honors its German culture with an annual Oktoberfest. The festival, held in October, is a celebration of German song, dance, and food.

The Tifton Native American Cultural Exchange holds an annual Native-American gathering at the end of March. Visitors can view early Native-American living structures that are on display.

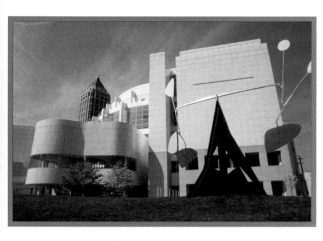

The High Museum of Art, built in 1983, has modern curves, sunny atriums, and spacious windows.

ARTS AND ENTERTAINMENT

Georgia's entertainment capital is the elegant city of Atlanta. The city boasts a High Museum of Art at the Woodruff Arts Center which displays a variety of folk art, photography, and other exhibits. The Woodruff Arts Center also houses a professional theater and a symphony orchestra. At the Clark Atlanta University, viewers can see a large collection of African-American art.

There are many arts and crafts festivals throughout the state. Most of Georgia's traditional arts and crafts culture comes from people of the northern mountain areas. Hiawassee and Tallulah Falls are famous for their art fairs and festivals. Many country fairs feature handiwork by local residents. People are eager to buy homemade blankets, weavings, and paintings produced by Georgia's communities.

QUICK FACTS

Panning for gold is an entertaining hobby at Dahlonega, a museum in northern Georgia. The area around the museum was once rich with gold nuggets.

In the north, Georgia holds country-music conventions, where musicians gather to play blues, country, and bluegrass music.

At the Cyclorama Building in Atlanta, visitors can see the largest mural in the world. The mural, which depicts the Battle of Atlanta, is over 350 feet long.

Today's basket weavers use the same techniques as those of the 1800s. They form the baskets by weaving flat strips of oak, called "splits," in and out of sixteen "ribs" that are spread in a circular shape on the ground.

Many southerners have found fame and fortune in Hollywood. Among Georgia's actors are Burt Reynolds, Miriam Hopkins, and Stacey Keach. DeForest Kelley, another Georgian, played the grouchy Dr. McCoy on *Star Trek*, one of the most popular television programs of all-time.

Georgia's long tradition of blues and country music has influenced generations of residents. Many great singers and musicians come from the state. Some of Georgia's earlier singers and musicians were Ray Charles, Gladys Knight, Blind Willie McTell, Otis Redding, and Little Richard. Today, Georgian singers entertain country-music audiences with their popular melodies. Both Trisha Yearwood and Travis Tritt come from this southern state. Yearwood had the honor of singing at the closing ceremonies for the 1996 Olympic Games.

Trisha Yearwood grew up in rural Monticello. She has won an American Music Award, three Grammy Awards, and many Country Music Association awards.

QUICK FACTS

Authors from Georgia include novelist Alice Walker, and poets James Dickey and Conrad Aiken.

Blind Willie McTell was an incredible musician. He developed his own finger-picking style on both six-string and twelve-string guitars. Blind Willie McTell played blues, ragtime, folk, and ballads.

Lawrence Fishburne III was born in Augusta. He has starred in such films as *What's Love Got to Do With It* and *The Matrix*.

Now a very popular form of music, the roots of blues can be traced back to southern plantations, like those in Georgia. Blues music rose out of the suffering of African-American slaves.

Carl Lewis was the second competitor in Olympic history to win a gold medal in the same event for four Olympic Games in a row.

SPORTS

Georgia's greatest sporting achievement was hosting the 1996 Summer Olympic Games. Georgia gained international acclaim when Atlanta won the Olympic bid. The city received much attention for its elaborate five-hour opening ceremonies, which ended with boxing-great Muhammad Ali lighting the Olympic Flame. Atlanta was in the spotlight for two weeks while athletes from around the world competed for medals.

The city of Atlanta spent nearly $1.7 billion on the Summer Olympics. Athletes competed in Atlanta's majestic Olympic Stadium. At the games, the United States's Carl Lewis won his ninth gold medal in track and field. The Atlanta Games are remembered for their country-fair atmosphere, complete with booths, amusement-park rides, and concerts.

QUICK FACTS

The city of Atlanta received $300 million from the Coca-Cola Company to help fund the 1996 Summer Olympic Games.

A bomb caused two deaths during the Olympic Games. No one has ever been found guilty of causing the explosion in Atlanta's Centennial Olympic Park.

Nature lovers can visit Georgia's fifty-nine state parks. Many of these have picnic areas, playgrounds, and cottages.

The Georgia Sports Hall of Fame honors great athletes from around the nation. Hall of Fame members include Hank Aaron and Ty Cobb.

To help create the spectacular opening ceremonies for the 1996 Summer Olympic Games in Atlanta, more than 5,000 costumes were made from 87 different designs.

In 1995, the Braves won their first World Series in Atlanta. They beat the Cleveland Indians 4 games to 2.

Georgia has four professional sports teams. The Atlanta Falcons play in the National Football League, while the Atlanta Braves compete in Major League Baseball. The Atlanta Thrashers brought professional hockey to Atlanta in the 1999–2000 season. The Atlanta Hawks represent Georgia in the National Basketball Association.

Atlanta's Olympic Stadium now serves as home to the Braves. Over the years, the Braves moved from Boston to Milwaukee, and then settled in Atlanta. In 1991, the Atlanta Braves made history when they became the first team to reach the World Series only one year after having the worst record in the league.

Georgia has a variety of activities for outdoor enthusiasts. The ocean attracts swimmers to its salty waters, and the mountains draw climbers to their rocky peaks. Hikers can visit a number of state parks and forests, including the Cohutta Wilderness Area in Chattahoochee National Forest.

The Ocoee River was used for the 1996 Olympic Games Whitewater Rafting Events. It offers two 5-mile sections of large drops, wild waves, and white-water rapids.

QUICK FACTS

The Atlanta Braves have had many different names over the years. They have been called the Red Stockings, the Beaneaters, the Doves, the Rustlers, and the Bees.

Finding it difficult to settle on one sport, Deion Sanders played baseball for the Atlanta Braves and football for the Atlanta Falcons.

The annual Masters Golf Tournament is played in Augusta. It begins the first week of April.

Brain Teasers

1

What is Georgia's most valuable crop?

a. Hay

b. Peanuts

c. Cotton

d. Corn

Answer: b. Peanuts. Georgia grows the most nuts and peanuts in the nation.

2

How did Blackbeard Island earn its name?

Answer: The island received its name from pirate Edward "Blackbeard" Teach, who made his home there.

3

Who was Mary Musgrove, and what did she do?

Answer: Mary Musgrove was a half-Creek, half-English woman who owned a trading post near Savannah. She helped keep the peace between Native Americans and colonists while serving as an interpreter.

4

Why is there a tree that owns itself in Georgia?

Answer: When Colonel William Jackson passed away in Athens in 1890, he willed his favorite childhood tree, along with the 8 feet of earth that surrounded it, to itself.

5

What does the word "Okefenokee" in Okefenokee Swamp mean?

Answer: Okefenokee is a Native-American word meaning "trembling earth." The term refers to the bushes and weeds that seem to "tremble" on top of the swamp's waters.

6

Why was a Georgia theme park named Six Flags Over Georgia?

Answer: The name refers to the six different flags that have flown over Georgia since the arrival of the Europeans. The six flags represent England, Spain, Liberty, Georgia, the Confederate States of America, and the United States of America.

7

What important United States Supreme Court decision occurred in 1954?

Answer: The United States Supreme Court declared that segregated schools were against the law. However, it was not until 1961 that Georgia's African-American students were able to attend non-segregated schools.

8

What is it illegal to do in Gainesville?

Answer: It is illegal to eat chicken with a fork in Gainesville. Gainesville is the "Chicken Capital of the World."

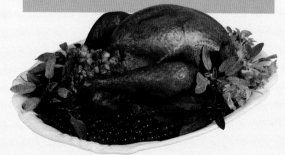

FOR MORE INFORMATION

Books

Aylesworth, Thomas G. and Virginia L. *The Southeast: Georgia, Kentucky, Tennessee*. New York: Chelsea House, 1995.

Coleman, Kenneth, ed. *A History of Georgia*. 2nd ed. Athens: University of Georgia Press, 1991.

Fradin, Dennis B. *Georgia*. Chicago: Children's Press, 1991.

LaDoux, Rita C. *Georgia*. Minneapolis: Lerner Publications, 1991.

Web sites

You can also go online and have a look at the following Web sites:

Georgia History
http://www.ngeorgia.com/history/early.html

50 States: Georgia
http://www.50states.com/georgia.htm

State of Georgia
http://www.state.ga.us/

Some Web sites stay current longer than others. To find other Georgia Web sites, enter search terms such as "Georgia," "Atlanta," "Martin Luther King Jr.," or any other topic you want to research.

GLOSSARY

atriums: glass-covered lobbies found in buildings

broiler chickens: chickens raised for their meat rather than their eggs

civil rights movement: the struggle in the 1950s and 1960s to provide racial equality for African Americans in the United States

convert: to change

descendants: relatives

endangered: in danger of becoming extinct

game: wild animals hunted for food or sport

hydroelectric: energy created from moving water

March to the Sea: a famous military action during the American Civil War when Union forces marched from Atlanta to Savannah

mercantilism: a system to keep money in one's own country

plantation: a large estate or farm on which crops such as cotton are grown

precipitation: rain, hail, or snow that falls to the ground

pulpwood: soft wood used to make paper

quarried: stone removed from an excavation pit

reservations: lands reserved for Native Americans

secede: to withdraw from an alliance

segregation: forcing separation and restrictions based on race

state chartered: created by the state through official documents

textile: fabric made by weaving or knitting

INDEX

American Civil War 6, 12
Andersonville National
  Historic Site 12
Athens 15, 22, 28
Atlanta 4, 5, 6, 7, 11, 12,
  14, 15, 20, 22, 21, 23,
  24, 26, 27
Atlanta Braves 27
Atlanta Falcons 27
Augusta 25, 27

Brasstown Bald Mountain
  5, 8

Carter, Jimmy 21
Chattahoochee National
  Forest 27
Chattahoochee River 5,
  20
Coca-Cola 14, 26
Cohutta Wilderness Area
  27
Columbus 20
Cyclorama Building 24

Fishburne III, Lawrence
  25

Jackson, Maynard 21

King Jr., Martin Luther 7,
  22

Lincoln, Abraham 7

McTell, Blind Willie 25
Musgrove, Mary 28

Native Americans (Native
  Peoples) 16, 17, 18,
  19, 20, 23, 28, 29

Ocmulgee National
  Monument 16
Oglethorpe, James Edward
  17, 19
Okefenokee Swamp 10,
  11, 29
Olympic Games 4, 21, 25,
  26, 27

Rock Eagle 16

Savannah 17, 18, 20, 28
Savannah River 5, 19
SciTrek 12
Sequoyah, Chief 17
Soto, Hernando de 18

Tubman African American
  Museum 22

University of Georgia 15